# Santa's Day Jobs

## By

## Larry L. Deibert

## Illustrated by

## Ashley Reigle

Copyright 2016

ISBN: 13-978-1537305738

Larry L. Deibert

All Rights Reserved

Thanks to Ashley Reigle

For her artistry

Thanks to best-selling author

Alaska Angelini

For completing the covers

Thanks to all the children who participated...

Thanks to my editors, my daughter, Laura Beck and my wife, Peggy Deibert

Thanks to Louise Williams, owner of Louise and Company for her input

# Introduction

One day, shortly before Christmas, 2015, I was working at my part-time job, when a little girl stared at me and then exclaimed, "Santa!"

Not knowing what to say to her, I just smiled and nodded, but she was the seed to a new idea-Santa's Day Jobs.

As the day progressed, I thought that this book could be a possibility because with today's technology, Santa certainly has a lot of free time. He can communicate with his elves using e-mail, text messaging, and face time.

For years, toys have been created using more automation than elf power and Justin, his chief elf, could oversee all facets of the toy-making, insuring that everything was ready by Christmas Eve.

After delivering all the toys and returning to the North Pole, Santa gave his wife a kiss and said, "In three days, I am leaving for a year's sabbatical from toy-making. I am going to see what people do for a living and I will work twelve jobs before I return."

Mrs. Claus simply nodded because she thought it was a great idea, too.

# Lifeguard Santa

Santa flew to Daytona Beach Florida to begin his year of day jobs.

The job of a lifeguard is very important, because it is his job to see to the safety of all swimmers and non-swimmers alike. It can be at a beach, a pool, or a lake, but first and foremost, the lifeguard makes sure everyone in the area is safe.

Lifeguards must be very good swimmers, physically fit (Oops, Santa, it appears as though you need to take off a few pounds this month.) and enjoy being near and in the water.

As first responders, they need to have a lot of medical knowledge and must be trained to perform CPR and treat cuts and burns, too.

A lifeguard sits on a watchtower, or a very tall chair, in order to see long distances both side to side and toward the water. The lifeguard could also have binoculars and a whistle to get the attention of swimmers and surfers to let them know they are out too far and to stop horseplay on the beach and in the water.

Like the water goers he protects, he must also use a lot of sunscreen to protect himself from the harmful rays of the sun. (Forgot your nose, Santa?)

Well, children, do you think Santa would be good as a lifeguard?

I think he will be happy to move on to his next job.

# School Bus Driver Santa

Because Santa loves children so much, he wanted to drive a school bus, transporting them to and from school safely. He also knew that there were many other responsibilities to doing the job.

Since he is known worldwide, the school district didn't feel he needed to go through background checks like other drivers. The school needs to know a driver's vehicle history; a school bus driver must have a clean driving record. The school district also checks to see that drivers have not broken any non-driving laws. Children need to be protected and these background checks help to keep them safe.

Santa did have to take driver training for large vehicles because his skill with a reindeer driven sleigh didn't count. Because of his magic, he was able to complete the training in an hour and received his license.

He also had to keep records of the number of students taken to and from school each day. He kept a log of miles driven and number of stops he made. Santa kept a record of the amount of gas he used each day. Although it never happened on his schedule, drivers had to keep records of any disciplinary action that had to be given to unruly riders. If necessary, he helped younger children cross the street.

When it was time to move on, Santa was given a safe driving certificate from the school district.

# Farmer Santa

There are many types of farms. Many grow different kinds of crops to feed America and the world. Some of the other kinds of farms are dairy farms, where cows are raised to provide the milk we need for drinking and to make other dairy products such as cheese and of course, Santa's favorite, ice cream.

Orchards provide our fruits. Other farms raise hogs, chickens and there are even fish farms. Special farms raise exotic animals and birds like buffalo and ostriches.

Santa chose to work on a farm that grew corn. Have you ever passed by huge fields of corn when you took a drive with your parents, relatives or friends?

Santa had to learn many things to raise a corn crop. A farmer has to know the best time of the year to plow the fields and plant the seeds. During dry periods plants have to be watered so they don't dry out and die and the farmer knows how much water to give the plants at different stages in their growth. Farmers have to know the length of the growing season in order to get the crops to market at the peak of freshness

Farmers often have long days, starting at sunrise and ending at sundown. No matter what kind of farm, there is always lots of work to do to provide what humans and animals need to survive.

# Baseball Catcher Santa

One of Santa's favorite sports is baseball and when he was offered a day job to catch for a minor league team, he immediately accepted the offer. After a couple of days of training, he was going to be put into the lineup and when he ran out onto the field and took his position behind the plate, the applause was the longest and loudest baseball fans around the world have ever heard. A mic was brought out to him and as the crowd quieted, he said, "I want to thank the Cardinals for giving me this opportunity and I will do my very best." Cheers erupted again and when the crowd sat back down, the umpire cried out, "Play ball."

Santa got in a crouch behind the plate and using his glove to block his signs being stolen, he gave the pitcher the sign for a fast ball and just before the pitch was to be thrown, he placed his glove where he wanted the ball to be thrown. The pitcher threw a strike and the game was on.

Over the course of the game, the catcher is the only player who can see everything that is going on across the whole field. On ground balls to the infield, he would jump up and take off toward first base to back up the first baseman on a throw-unless an opposing player was on third base. He would then have to be prepared to take a throw to the plate.

When he would tear off his mask to catch a foul ball, his Santa hat would always manage to stay on his head. He played hard every game he was in and when his month was over, he was given a golden catcher's mitt for having no errors.

Children and adults alike, both viewing in the stadium or on their TV screens loved every moment of watching baseball catcher Santa.

# Teacher Santa

Santa loves children so much, he was very happy when a school offered him a teaching job for a month. He would be teaching third grade.

To become a teacher, you should have really good grades, especially in high school. You should also score well in your SAT which all colleges look at for admission. Once admitted, someone learning how to be a teacher will go for four years to earn a Bachelor's Degree in Education. Fortunately, Santa did not have to go to college because his magic allowed him to know every aspect of teaching.

A teacher must have great communication skills in order to give students, parents, and staff information: to have them understand everything that is being taught, especially considering the great diversity of students. Santa will teach them math, reading, social studies and science. The students will take work home in third grade, where parents will help them to better their study habits.

Santa will also use his skills of creativity, of which he has many, to instruct students to use their minds in many ways. He must also have the ability to handle any situation that may come up in third grade and he will also need great energy to keep up with his students.

In many schools, third grade teachers also have to be bilingual to help students who speak Spanish or other languages.

One of Santa's favorite parts of teaching was when he had the opportunity to read to his students and then have a discussion about the book.

# Letter Carrier Santa

Santa completed the postal exam, Exam 473, the test all prospective carriers must take to get a job.

A letter carrier clocks in at his or her starting time, goes out to the parking lot and physically checks the vehicle he or she will be using. Each route has an assigned vehicle, unless it is in the garage being worked on, then the carrier must use a spare vehicle.

Santa physically checked the vehicle for any damage that may not have been there the day before. He also looked at the tires to see that they were properly inflated. He unlocked the door and checked the turn signals, having to get out to see if the rear signals were working. He also turned on the lights to make sure they were working. Finally he started the truck to make sure it was running properly. He locked the door and went back inside to his letter carrier case.

He spent the next hour or so inserting letter size and larger mail, called flats, into slots that corresponded with the address on the mail piece. Once all the available mail he could carry in his eight hour day was cased, he got his accountable mail, mail that he had to sign for, and that the customer would have to sign for as well, and his special key that fit every mailbox in the city and the apartment or business boxes where he would have to place the customer's mail.

He got his hamper, sorted his packages and pulled all the mail from his case, in delivery order, placing the mail in trays and then putting the trays in the hamper. Once finished with that, he took the hamper to his truck, loaded, returned the hamper and then finally left for the route to deliver his mail. Today, his friend Susie wanted to show him the letter carrier outfit her mom made for her and to have her picture taken with Santa.

# Soldier Santa

In order to become a soldier, you must first go to see a recruiter. You and the recruiter will discuss what jobs are available, based on your education to this point in time. He will ask you many questions and you will have many questions for your recruiter as well. If you are qualified, both physically and mentally, you will be given a report date to a Basic Combat Training (BCT) facility.

In basic training you will learn what you need to become a soldier. Over a ten week period, you will take written tests, get a military style haircut, uniforms, and learn how to interact with recruits of many ethnic backgrounds. You will learn how to properly make a bunk and keep all of your things in order in your lockers.

You will learn the many skills you will need to be a soldier including firing different weapons, map reading, and physical fitness-you will exercise every day. A recruit will march almost everywhere he or she goes-to classrooms, mess hall (this is the military version of a cafeteria), outdoor classes, weapon ranges, and back again. You will run obstacle courses and learn how to defeat enemy soldiers with your skills.

At the end of BCT, you will be assigned your AIT (advanced individual training) unless you have already chosen a military job with your recruiter.

Your AIT will last from 8 to 10 weeks and you will learn everything there is to know about doing that specific job.

Once your training is complete, you will be assigned to one of a great many military bases all over the world.

# Chef Santa

There are many kinds of chefs. Pastry chefs prepare all the pastries; pantry chefs are in charge of cold foods and salads. Sauté chefs work at the sauté stations, where they quickly cook and brown foods for further preparation. Grill chefs will cook the foods that need to be grilled. At some buffets there are chefs who only prepare eggs to the customer's specifications. Santa loves omelet chefs who prepare his ham, onion, mushroom and cheese omelets.

The job of being a chef can be very challenging. A chef must stay on his feet for hours on end in sometimes cramped, hot, and humid kitchens. They also must deal with stressful situations. If a customer does not like how his food is cooked, the waitress or waiter will bring it back to the chef to either be completely recooked or just cooked a little bit.

Chefs need to have good taste buds and put the food on a plate so that it presents a good appearance.

Some chefs attend a culinary academy to learn their trade while others begin working in a restaurant and work their way up through the many different jobs in a kitchen until they have all the knowledge and work experience to become a chef.

Catering chefs prepare food at their kitchen and deliver the meals to the clients. A personal chef prepares and serves the meals in the client's home.

Santa is preparing a soup, while his assistant is making cookies. Be careful, Santa: it appears as though your soup is overcooking.

# Dog Groomer Santa

A new dog groomer usually learns the job by working with experienced groomers. He or she may help to keep the animals under control, cleaning up after the dog is groomed, and cleaning all the equipment a groomer uses and answering phone-in appointments. If a groomer wants to become licensed, he or she must complete a master grooming certification program.

The job of a groomer is to improve the dog's appearance by washing, cutting and trimming the dog's fur. A groomer will also trim the dog's nails, if needed, and will check the dog's teeth to see if there is any decay to tell the owner about. The groomer will use many different tools to complete the job properly.

Today, Santa is grooming Riley, a 35 pound Springer/Lab. Riley has always been a good dog every time he has been groomed, so Santa should have no problems.

Santa lifts Riley up onto a metal table and he shampoos Riley's fur, being careful not to get any soap in the dog's eyes. He pays special attention to Riley's undercarriage, which is what Riley's owner calls his belly. After washing him, Santa dries him off with a hair blower and then he cuts and trims the coat. Riley's nails are a little long, so he trims them with a special clipper.

After finishing the job, Santa puts a bandana around Riley's neck and gives him a couple of treats. Riley responds by giving Santa a 'snookie' which is a dog kiss and soon his owner, Larry, takes him home.

# Doctor Santa

Again, because Santa loves children, he is going to spend a month working with a local pediatrician. Pediatricians treat children for Illnesses and injuries, infections, childhood diseases and minor infections.

Pediatricians take care of infants, and children usually until they become young adults and wish to begin seeing a general practitioner. To become a pediatrician, Doctor Jones had to go to four years of college, plus four years of medical school. After graduating, Dr. Jones served as a pediatric resident, where he worked with pediatric physicians for three years. He then got his license to practice pediatric medicine.

Susie came to see Dr. Jones and Dr. Santa because she fell off her bike and broke her wrist. They gave her a physical exam, including several sets of x-rays to see how badly her wrist was fractured. Dr. Santa told her that he would have to reset the break and that it might hurt a little. He gave her anesthesia before doing the procedure – this is used to numb the pain.

Susie awakened to see that he had placed her wrist in a cast. She will have to wear the cast for six to eight weeks as her wrist heals. During that time period, more x-rays will be taken to see that the wrist is healing properly. She smiled when she saw that he signed her cast.

Susie was very happy to have been treated by Santa Claus and Dr. Jones.

Eight weeks later, Santa had moved on to a new day job and Dr. Jones removed her cast. Her wrist had healed perfectly. Before she was released, she received a phone call from Santa congratulating her on being a great patient.

# Hairdresser Santa

The crowd of children waiting outside the door of Louise and Company, in Allentown, Pennsylvania, cheered as soon as they saw a limousine pull up and Santa stepped out.

The children entered the shop in threes, one child per chair. Santa was equipped with a pair of scissors and a clipper. He had a hair dryer strapped to a belt with a holster, especially made by him and for him in which to keep the dryer when not in use.

When the three children, two girls and a boy were seated, Santa rubbed his stomach and said some strange words, enabling him to use his magic. As he finished cutting one child's hair, that child would leave and another would take his or her place. Santa's hands flew over the heads of the children, giving them perfect cuts in no more than a minute. His magic allowed him to know exactly how to cut each head of hair, and blow dry the hair in no more than a minute. Louise and parents alike were totally amazed to see this.

When the children left the shop, they were greeted by Santa's helper, Ashley, who gave them each a lollipop

Louise told Santa some things about her life as a hairstylist. She trained at Empire Beauty School. She worked in a salon for 2years, first as a shampoo person, then as a skin tech. Louise also did manicures and pedicures. The second year she moved to a different salon and was hired as Manager, Stylist, and Nail Tech. After 2 years she left there and opened her first salon, Designers International and ran that for 14 years. She worked at another salon for 4 years before opening Louise and Company 8 years ago. "The best thing about my profession is that I have watched kids grow up and now I am cutting the hair of their kids. I just love that about my job!" she exclaimed.

# Astronaut Santa

Since our space program began in 1959, when NASA selected our first astronauts to train, 335 Americans have gone into space, with 12 of them having walked on the moon. Neil Armstrong and Buzz Aldrin were the first two Americans to leave their footprints on the moon on July 20th, 1969. Alan Shepard was the only astronaut to play golf on the moon, hitting two golf balls on February 6th, 1971.

To become an astronaut, military applicants go through their branch of service to apply while civilians, people not in the military, apply to NASA directly. NASA is the National Aeronautics and Space Administration. Candidates must have an educational background that includes a bachelor's degree in either physical science, mathematics, engineering or biological science.

If you want to be the pilot of a spacecraft, you must have at least 1000 hours as a pilot in jet aircraft, be between 5 feet 2 inches and 6 feet 3 inches tall with 20/100 uncorrected vision corrected to 20/20 with eyewear. Sitting blood pressure should be 140 over 90 or better.

Santa passed the eye test and his blood pressure was fine so he was given the go to go up in space and walk in space which was something he wanted to do ever since Ed White walked in space on June 3rd. 1965.

After orbiting the earth, giving Santa a view of the entire planet, he was suited up and stepped into space wearing a tether that kept him from floating away.

After returning back to earth, Santa was given a huge sendoff by NASA employees as he hopped in his sleigh to head back to the North Pole. Christmas was only ten days away.

# Santa Claus

Well-known throughout the world, Santa has many names He is known as Saint Nicholas, Saint Nick, Father Christmas, and Kris Kringle

Whatever name you call him is not important; what is important is that he delivers gifts to good boys and girls every Christmas Eve.

Although Christmas is the day we celebrate the birth of Jesus Christ, the spirt of Christmas is often passed from the joy of children to their parents, relatives and friends and most people feel really good at this time of the year.

He delivers the gifts and toys with the help of his elves, eight flying reindeer and a magic bag that never empties until each child is visited by this jolly old elf.

We can be so thankful that there is such a person as Santa, even though few people see him delivering the toys and gifts.

I wish I could explain how he gets down those chimneys and the other methods he uses to gain entrance to homes that have no fireplaces, but that is the magic of Santa.

So, Ashley and I hope that you will hang your stockings where Santa can find them; listen to your parents and teachers, and be good boys and girls so that you will get a visit from St. Nick.

Ashley and I  hope you enjoyed reading Santa's Day Jobs.

# About the author

Larry L. Deibert is a retired letter carrier and he is the author of many books; The Christmas City Vampire, Combat Boots dainty feet-Finding Love In Vietnam, The Other Side Of The Ridge-Gettysburg, June 27th 2013 to July 2nd 1863, Fathoms, From Darkness To Light, Family, and The Life Of Riley. Santa's Day Jobs is his first illustrated children's book.

Larry and his wife, Peggy, love to travel, especially to Wrightsville Beach, North Carolina. Both love to read and spend time with their granddaughter. Larry is a terrible golfer but he still loves to play.

## About the illustrator

Ashley Reigle, is a freelance artist and licensed cosmetologist, living in the Center Valley area. Originally from Illinois, Ashley enjoys spending time with her husband Timothy, who is a funeral director in the area. She also spends a great deal of her time taking care of her two beautiful daughters, Lorelei and Addison. Ashley loves sharing her gift with her girls, who are great at art as well. She is thrilled to be able to share her gift with children everywhere through the illustrations in this book.

# Santa's Day Jobs
# Coloring Book

Children, this coloring book gives you the opportunity to color the pictures like Ashley colored them, or use your imagination and change the colors to your liking.

Ashley and I hope you will enjoy coloring these pictures.

# Lifeguard Santa

Ella-When people are drowning, they help them and take them out of the water

Remy-Lifeguards keep people safe from not drowning.

Jenny-They can help people learn how to swim and do cool things in the water.

Sophia Elizabeth Minor-To make sure people are safe in the pool but having fun.

Brayden Shoemaker-Keeps you safe.

Hannah Wargo-Make sure that people don't drown in the water.

# School Bus Driver Santa

Nick-A bus driver takes kids to school and home from school.

Ryan-They tell you to sit down when you ride a bus.

Sophia Elizabeth Minor-They drive kids to school.

Brayden Shoemaker-Gets you to school.

Hannah Wargo-Drives kids to school in a big bouncy bus so they can learn from their teachers.

# Farmer Santa

Andrew-The farmer gets crops from the ground, and gives them to the chef to make food.

Lara-A farmer is someone who takes care of animals on a farm and he grows food in his garden.

Sophia Elizabeth Minor-They clean pigs and cows and dogs and ducks and chickens and hens. I'm not a farmer because remember I don't have a dog.

Brayden Shoemaker-A farmer keeps his animals and takes good care of them.

Hannah Wargo-Takes care of the animals and grows vegetables for everyone to eat and be healthy.

# Baseball Catcher Santa

**None of the children submitted a response for this day job.**

# Teacher Santa

Veronica-They help kids learn all kinds of stuff and they really want them to keep trying so they can do their best.

Sean-Teachers teach kids not to bully.

Jenny-Teachers help people learn how to do addition, subtraction, multiplication and division.

Cienna Smith-My teacher helps all of us in the classroom get ready for third grade. She does crafts with us and she is fun to be with. She even lets us sit by our friends in class. She lets us play games with math and that is fun. She is the best teacher.

Sophia Elizabeth Minor-Teaches kids in a classroom how to read and they can do that because of their teachers.

Brayden Shoemaker-They teach you math and let you eat lunch in the cafeteria.

Hannah Wargo-Helps us understand right from wrong. We learn things so we can be smart and get a good job when we grow up.

# Letter Carrier Santa

Jules-He goes around on bikes and throws your mail on the driveway.

Noah-Mail carriers keep you connected to what is happening by delivering letters and information

Sophia Elizabeth Minor-They drive around town handing out mail. They work so hard, but sometimes they bring bills which you know grownups don't like.

Brayden Shoemaker-Delivers letters to you.

Hannah Wargo-Delivers mail...even in the rain and snow, and it's usually bills or magazines.

# Soldier Santa

Andrew-Their job is to protect the US and fight in battles so we can be free.

Emil-They help the country stay safe.

Owen-A soldier is someone who fights for their country.

Sophia Elizabeth Minor-They fight for our country so we can be free and enjoy our families even when they can't.

Brayden Shoemaker-A soldier protects our state.

Hannah Wargo-Saves the world from bad people.

# Chef Santa

Abby-A chef is someone who works at a restaurant. They make really good food and you have to go to a special school to learn how to do that.

Veronica-A chef teaches people how to cook for their families and they cook really good stuff, and they work really hard.

Sean-A chef makes really good food for very important people.

Danielle-Someone who cooks stuff for you if you don't have time to cook it yourself.

Sophia Elizabeth Minor-A chef cooks for people. Cooks what they ask for and asks them if they want dessert when they are done.

Brayden Shoemaker-He cooks food, like pizza and French fries and cookies.

Hannah Wargo-Cooks lots of yummy things for people at a restaurant.

# Dog Groomer Santa

Remy-Dog groomers cut dogs' hair and make them look pretty.

Jules-They cut the hair on dogs and wash them.

Sophia Elizabeth Minor-I don't know because I don't have a dog, but they probably play.

Brayden Shoemaker-A dog groomer cuts the dog's hair if it's too long.

Hannah Wargo-Wash and cut dogs' hair and put pretty bandanas or bows on them.

# Doctor Santa

Veronica-When people are sick, doctors keep the kids safe from germs and diseases. They care for kids so they can get better soon.

Lara-A doctor is someone who fixes people if they have a broken leg, if they're injured, they're feeling sick, or if they need care.

Sophia Elizabeth Minor-They make sure people are healthy and help people when they are sick by feeling and seeing.

Brayden Shoemaker-A doctor looks at your bones and helps you feel better.

Hannah Wargo-Checks out people who are hurt or sick and makes them better.

# Hairdresser Santa

Nick-They make your hair look pretty and fabulous.

Ava-They make your hair all fancy and the way you want it to be.

Danielle-A hairdresser does your hair in cool ways you don't know how to do.

Sophia Elizabeth Minor-They make peoples' hair pretty by using the stuff.

Brayden Shoemaker-They cut your hair.

Hannah Wargo-They make girls' hair look pretty and cut boys' hair so it's out of their faces.

# Astronaut Santa

Zach-They explore space and go on different planets.

Remy-When they are in space and have a problem, their crew helps them get back to earth.

Dennis-Astronauts can fly to Mars or the Moon.

Lara-An astronaut is someone who gets to fly into space. Since there's no gravity, they have fun walking around. They go back to America and tell people cool facts about what they found.

Sophia Elizabeth Minor-An astronaut flies to outer space to see if the planets are breaking or not breaking. Also to see how cold and hot they are.

Brayden Shoemaker-He goes out to space.

Hannah Wargo-He flies a big rocket into space and visits planets.

# Santa Claus

I want to thank all the children who participated in the Santa Day Jobs coloring book section. I appreciate all of your answers.

Here are the participants again.

From Karen Scheuer's Second Grade Class, 2015-16, Churchville Elementary:

Zach, Remy, Dennis, Lara, Abby, Veronica, Sean, Danielle, Jules, Andrew, Nick, Ava, Ella, Jenny, Noah, Ryan, Owen, and Emil.


Other participants:

Cienna Smith

Sophia Elizabeth Minor

Brayden Shoemaker

Hannah Wargo

**This was my original letter requesting help from kids. Please keep watching my Facebook page because it is possible that Ashley and I will do a new book for 2017 and I will need your help again. Thanks.**

*Larry L. Deibert, author from Hellertown, Pa. Seeking Help from your children to create a new book*

*Santa's Day Jobs*

*I need help. I am looking for kids 6-10 to offer their job descriptions of the following occupations; Astronaut, Chef, Doctor, Dog Groomer, Farmer, Hairstylist, Lifeguard, Letter Carrier, School Bus Driver, Soldier, Teacher. I am working on my first illustrated children's book titled Santa's Day Jobs. The first part will be illustrations of Santa in each job, followed by text by me describing the jobs so that children can understand. The second part of the book will be the sketches for kids to color and the text will be provided by your children. I will award a free copy to the best description of each job, although I will include as many descriptions as I can. If you are interested please send your child(s) descriptions to me larrydeibert@rcn.com Thanks.*